ANDREA CAPPELLARI

FIRST BOOK
OF CLASSICAL CLARINET

CLARINET

To access companion recorded accompaniments
online, visit:
www.halleonard.com/mylibrary

Enter Code
3016-5383-3727-8779

ISBN 978-1-5400-5462-3

RICORDI

EXCLUSIVELY DISTRIBUTED BY

Visit Hal Leonard Online at
www.halleonard.com

Contact us:
Hal Leonard
7777 West Bluemound Road
Milwaukee, WI 53213
Email: info@halleonard.com

In Europe, contact:
Hal Leonard Europe Limited
42 Wigmore Street
Marylebone, London, W1U 2RN
Email: info@halleonardeurope.com

In Australia, contact:
Hal Leonard Australia Pty. Ltd.
4 Lentara Court
Cheltenham, Victoria, 3192 Australia
Email: info@halleonard.com.au

Andrea Cappellari holds degrees in choral music and choral conducting, music education, and percussion instruments from the Giuseppe Verdi Conservatory in Milan. He is a lecturer at the Giacomo Puccini Higher Institute of Music Studies in Gallarate, Varese, Italy, and at the Candiani-Bausch High School of the Arts in Busto Arsizio, Varese, Italy. He teaches training and continuing education courses for teachers and courses in rhythm and ensemble music in French-speaking Switzerland. He is a director of choral and instrumental ensembles, and author of numerous educational publications andcollections of children's songs.

In memory of my beloved mother Wanda.

Thanks to Greta Ferrario

Cover Art by Giuseppe Spada

INTRODUCTION

First Book of Classical Clarinet is an invaluable collection of 100 melodies, ordered by progressive difficulty and intended for the beginning clarinetist.

First Book of Classical Clarinet is an absolute novelty in the teaching literature for the clarinet. Teachers and students will be able to use the material as a compliment to traditional methods.

The use of this anthology, enriched by piano accompaniments, will allow an immediate approach to ensemble music, encouraging the development of listening and musical interaction.

Enrico Maria Baroni

first clarinet of the National Symphony Orchestra of RAI, Torino, Italy

CONTENTS

MELODIES INDEXED BY COMPOSER

1 **Melodies of 3 Notes/Rhythmic Values:** 𝅝 𝅗𝅥. 𝅗𝅥 ♩

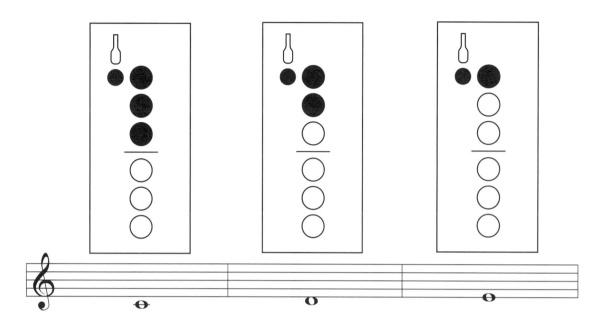

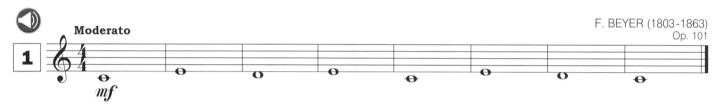

F. BEYER (1803-1863)
Op. 101

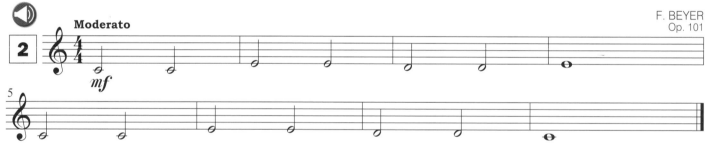

F. BEYER
Op. 101

F. BEYER
Op. 101

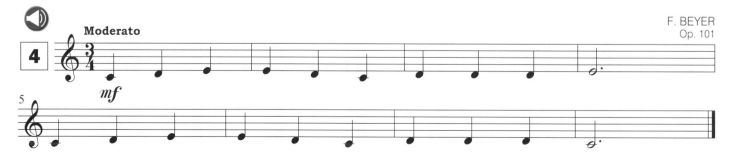

F. BEYER
Op. 101

F. BEYER
Op. 101

F. BEYER
Op. 101

F. BEYER
Op. 101

F. LISZT (1811-1886)
Pater noster

2 Melodies of 4 Notes/Rhythmic Values: o 𝅝. 𝅗𝅥 𝅘𝅥

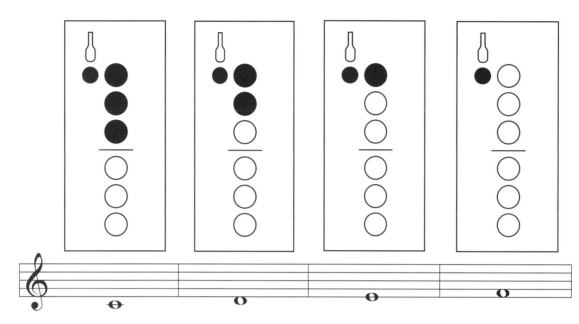

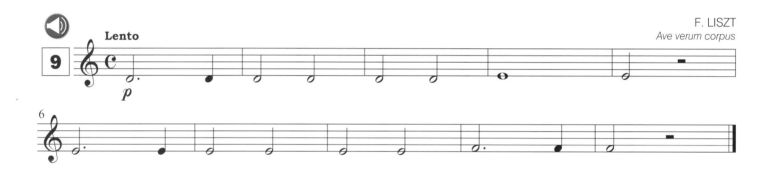

F. LISZT
Ave verum corpus

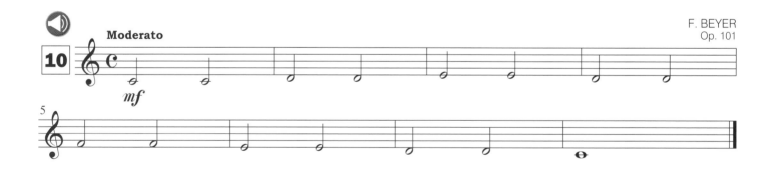

F. BEYER
Op. 101

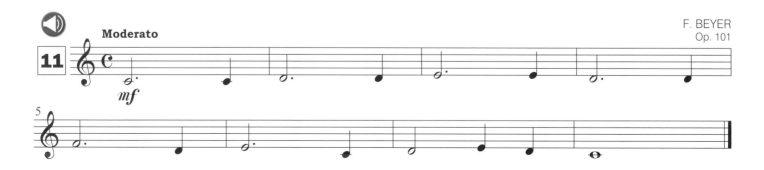

F. BEYER
Op. 101

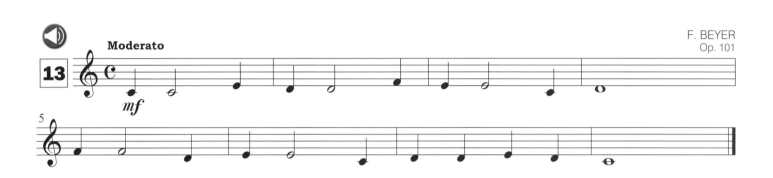

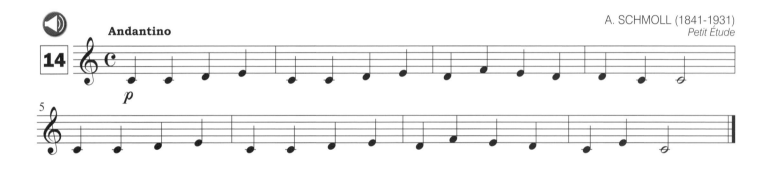

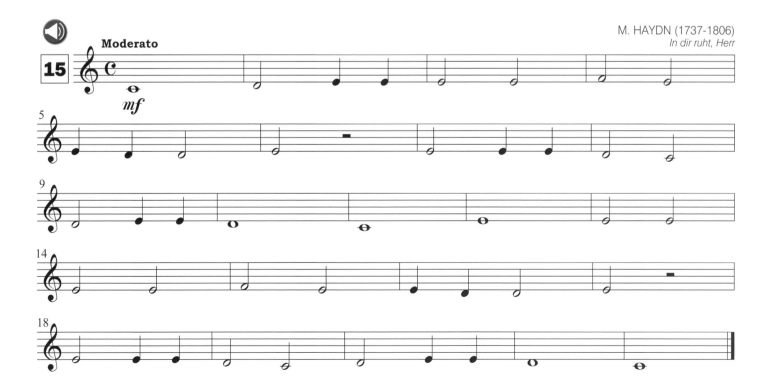

3 **Melodies of 5 Notes/Rhythmic Values:** o ♩. ♩ ♪

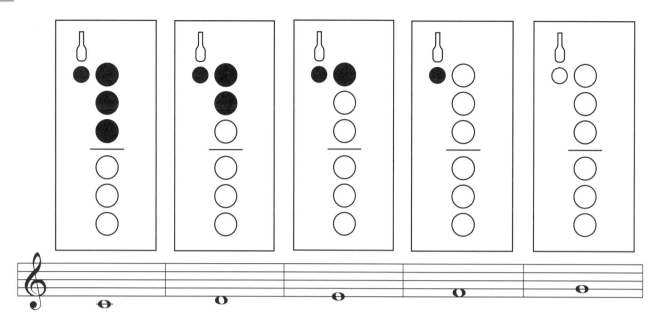

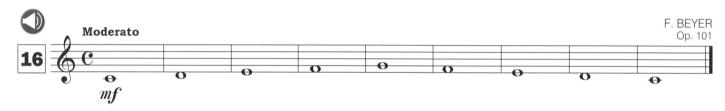

F. BEYER
Op. 101

16 Moderato

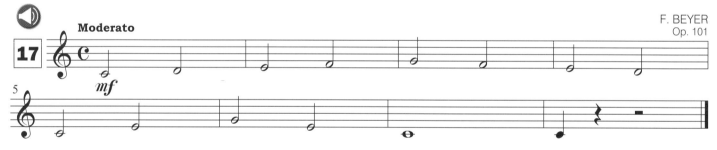

F. BEYER
Op. 101

17 Moderato

F. BEYER
Op. 101

18 Moderato

F. BEYER
Op. 101

19 Moderato

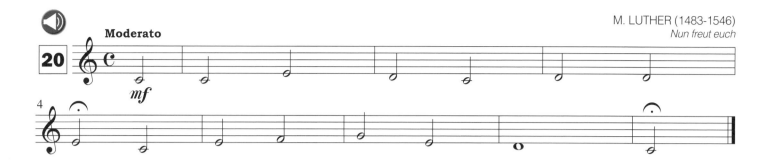

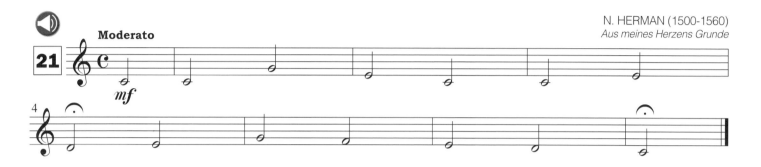

Melodies of 5 Notes/Rhythmic Values: from o to ♪

Preparatory Exercises

Allegretto

26

Vivace

27

Moderato

28

Moderato

29

5 Melodies of 6 Notes/Rhythmic Values: from 𝅝 to ♪

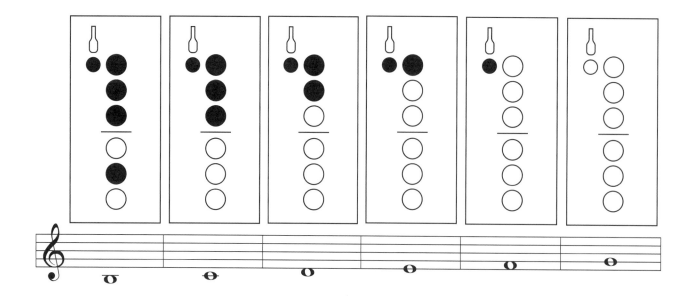

P.B. GRUBER (1759 -1796)
Ave Regina coelorum

Andante

30

5

D. BUXTEHUDE (1637-1707)
Sinfonia: *Du Friedefürst*

[Moderato]

31

6

12

17

23

Andantino

32

Andante

33

Menuetto grazioso

34

6 | Melodies of 5 Notes/Rhythmic Values: from 𝅝 to ♪

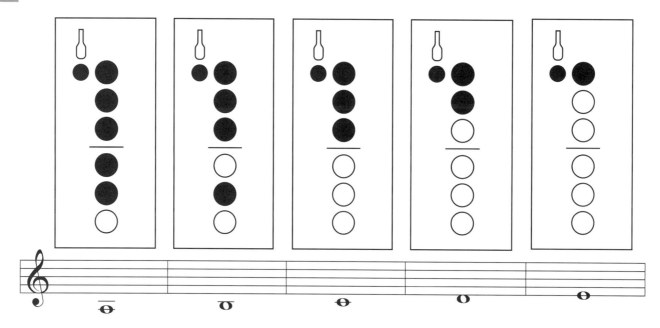

F. BEYER
Op. 101

35 Allegretto

F. BEYER
Op. 101

36 Andante

G. GASTOLDI (1555-1622)
La cortigiana

37 [Andante moderato]

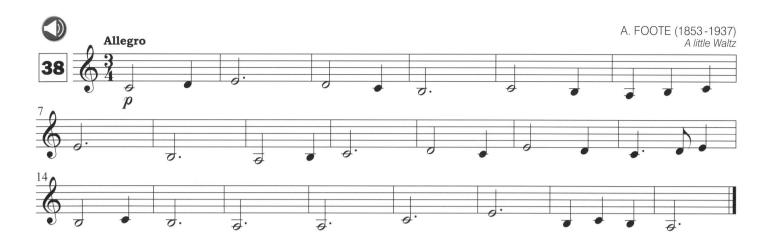

A. FOOTE (1853-1937)
A little Waltz

38 Allegro

D. MANZOLO (17th century)

39 [Moderato]

A. DIABELLI (1781-1858)
Alla turca

40 Allegro

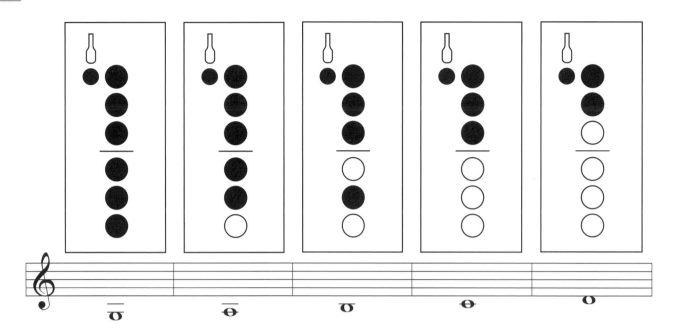

A. FOOTE
Quite contented

41 Andante con moto

K.M. KUNZ (1812-1875)
Canon

42 Con moto

A. CORELLI (1653-1713)
Concerto grosso n. 1

G.F. HANDEL
Concerto grosso Op. 6 n. 11

A. SCHMOLL
Petit Étude

A. FOOTE
Waltz

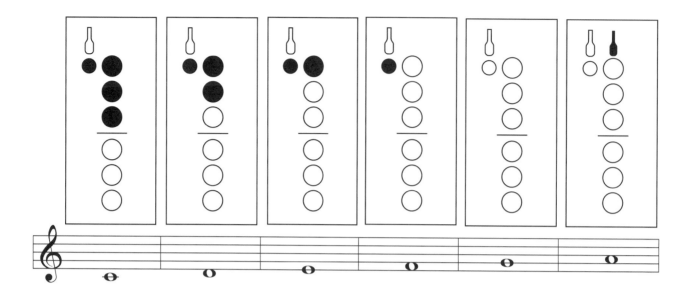

M. BERINGER (1580-1632)
Canon

47

M. BERINGER
Canon

48

9 Lento

10 Moderato

F. BEYER Op. 101

11 Moderato

F. BEYER Op. 101

12 Moderato

F. BEYER Op. 101

13 Moderato

F. BEYER Op. 101

14 Andantino

A. SCHMOLL (1841-1931) *Petit Étude*

15 Moderato

M. HAYDN (1737-1806) *In dir ruht, Herr*

16 Moderato

F. BEYER Op. 101

17 Moderato

F. BEYER Op. 101

18 Moderato

F. BEYER Op. 101

19 Moderato

F. BEYER Op. 101

20 Moderato

M. LUTHER (1483-1546) *Nun freut euch*

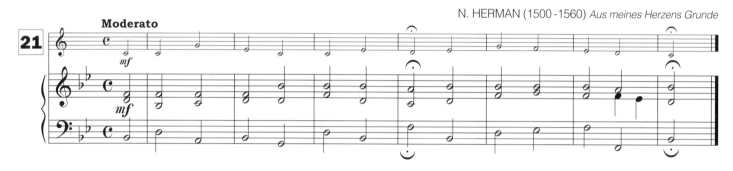

21 Moderato

N. HERMAN (1500-1560) *Aus meines Herzens Grunde*

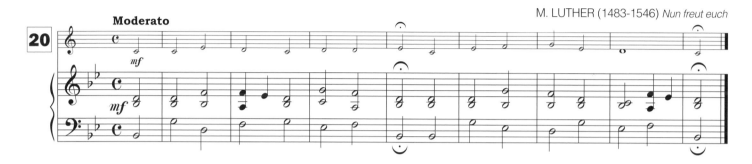

22 Moderato

F. BEYER Op. 101

23 A tempo giusto

G.F. HANDEL (1685-1759) *Sing ye to the Lord (Israel in Aegypt)*

12

C. CZERNY (1791-1857) Op. 777

24 Allegro

F. BEYER Op. 101

25 Comodo

W.A. MOZART (1756-1791) *Menuetto* (Serie 24 n. 58)

26 Allegretto

27 Vivace

A. CAMPRA (1660-1744) *Jubilate Deo*

28 Moderato

M. HAYDN *Kommt, ihr Christen*

29 Moderato

C. GEIST (1640-1711) *Verbum caro*

30 Andante

P.B. GRUBER (1759-1796) *Ave Regina coelorum*

[Moderato]

D. BUXTEHUDE (1637-1707) Sinfonia: *Du Friedefürst*

31

Andantino

M. GIULIANI (1781-1829) Op. 50 n. 1

32

33 Andante M.A. CHARPENTIER (1636-1704) *Klein Te Deum*

34 Menuetto grazioso I. PLEYEL (1757-1831) *Sonatina n. 6*

35 Allegretto *Fine* F. BEYER Op. 101

D.C. al Fine

36 Andante F. BEYER Op. 101

[Andante moderato]

G. GASTOLDI (1555-1622) *La Cortigiana*

Allegro

A. FOOTE (1853-1937) *A little Waltz*

[Moderato]

D. MANZOLO (17th century)

Largo

A. CORELLI (1653-1713) *Concerto grosso n. 1*

Andante

G.F. HANDEL *Concerto grosso* Op. 6 n. 11

Animato

A. SCHMOLL *Petit Étude*

Andantino

A. FOOTE *Waltz*

49 Brillante e vivace

J. BRAHMS (1833-1897) *Schönster Schats*

50 Allegro moderato

F. MENDELSSOHN (1809-1847) *Laudate pueri*

51 Maestoso ma non lento

C. FRANCK (1822-1890) *Dextera Domini*

52 Moderato

W.L. HAYDEN (1839-1886) *Waltz*

13

53 **Moderato** — B. SMETANA (1824-1884)

54 **Moderato** — F. BEYER Op. 101

55 **[Andante]** — Anonymous (18th century) *Magnificat*

56 **[Andante]** — W.A. MOZART *Minuetto* (Symphony n. 35)

57 **Allegro** — C. CZERNY Op. 777

58 **Melodioso** — E. GRANADOS (1867-1916) *Waltz*

14

59 Presto — A. DVOŘÁK (1841-1904) *Slavonic Dance* Op. 46 n. 1

60 Non troppo veloce — M.A. CHARPENTIER *Vous qui désirez sans fin*

61 Moderato — J. PACHELBEL (1653-1706) *Gott ist unser Zuversicht*

62 Adagio religioso — J. BERANEK (1813-1875) *Pater noster*

63 Molto allegro — W.A. MOZART *Quartet* K. 387

W.A. MOZART *Concerto for piano and orchestra* K. 537 n. 26 *("Coronation")*

64 Larghetto

N. PORPORA (1686 - 1768) *Concerto IV*

65 Allegro

W.A. MOZART *Deutsche Tänze* - Serie 11 n. 13

66 Allegro

H. PURCELL (1659 - 1695) *A new Irish tune*

70 Moderato

W.A. MOZART *Deutsche Tänze* - Serie 11 n. 13

71 [Allegro]

72 Andante

A. FOOTE *Reverie*

73 Presto

J. ROSENMÜLLER (1619-1684) *Meine Seele harret auf Gott*

74 Lento

M.A. CHARPENTIER *Domine Deus (Messe de minuit)*

76 Allegretto

C. CZERNY Op. 777

17

77 Allegro moderato

C. GOUNOD (1818-1893) *Gloria (Missa brevis)*

78 Comodo

F. BEYER Op. 101

80 Moderato

F. SCHUBERT (1797-1886) *Tänze Serie 12 n. 1*

81 Andante

W.L. HAYDEN *Rondò*

83 Moderato

F. BEYER Op. 101

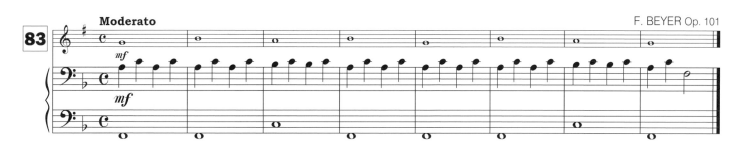

89 Un poco animato

A. SCHMOLL *Petit Étude*

90 Assai vivo

A. SCHMOLL *Petit Étude*

91 [Allegretto]

M. CORRETTE (1707-1795) *Menuet allemand*

92 Andantino

G. LANGE (1830 -1889) *Arietta - Sonatina* Op. 114 n. 4

93 Andante non troppo

C. FRANCK *Domine non secundum*

I. PLEYEL *Sonatina n. 1*

94 **Moderato**

mf

A. SCHMOLL
En prière

99 **Lento**

p *simile*

F. BURGMÜLLER (1806-1874) *Ave Maria*

100 **Andantino**

p

6 Moderato F. BEYER Op. 101

7 Moderato F. BEYER Op. 101

8 Lento F. LISZT (1811-1886) *Pater noster*

FIRST BOOK OF CLASSICAL CLARINET

F. BEYER (1803-1863) Op. 101

F. BEYER Op. 101

F. BEYER Op. 101

F. BEYER Op. 101

F. BEYER Op. 101

Brillante e vivace

J. BRAHMS (1833-1897)
Schönster Schats

Allegro moderato

F. MENDELSSOHN (1809-1847)
Laudate pueri

Maestoso ma non lento

C. FRANCK (1822-1890)
Dextera Domini

Moderato

W.L. HAYDEN (1839-1886)
Waltz

Moderato

B. SMETANA (1824-1884)

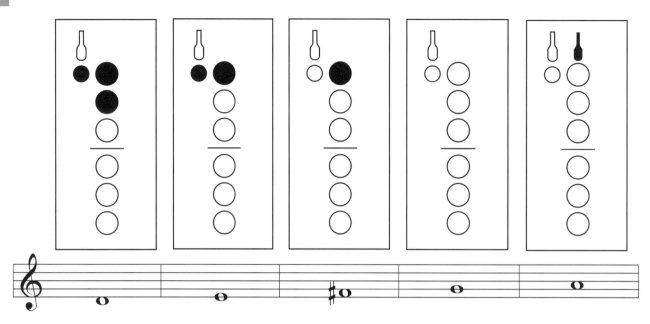

F. BEYER
Op.101

54 Moderato

mf

Anonymous (18th century)
Magnificat

55 [Andante]

mf

W.A. MOZART
Minuetto (Symphony n. 35)

56 [Andante]

p

C. CZERNY
Op. 777

57 Allegro

p

10 G-Major Scale

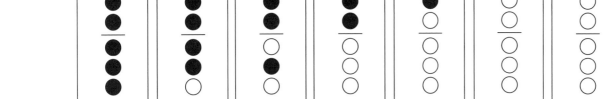

E. GRANADOS (1867-1916)
Waltz

58 **Melodioso**

A. DVOŘÁK (1841-1904)
Slavonic Dance Op. 46 n. 1

59 **Presto**

M.A. CHARPENTIER
Vous qui désirez sans fin

60 **Non troppo veloce**

J. PACHELBEL (1653-1706)
Gott ist unser Zuversicht

61 Moderato

J. BERANEK (1813-1875)
Pater noster

62 Adagio religioso

W.A. MOZART
Quartet K 387

63 Molto allegro

W.A. MOZART
Concerto for piano and orchestra K 537 n. 26 ("Coronation")

64 Larghetto

N. PORPORA (1686-1768)
Concerto IV

65 Allegro

W.A. MOZART
Deutsche Tänze - Serie 11 n. 13

66 **Allegro**

N. PORPORA
Concerto IV

67 **Andante**

B. GALUPPI (1706 - 1785)
Kyrie (Missa in Do)

68 **Moderato**

B. GALUPPI
Sanctus (Missa in Do)

69 **Lento**

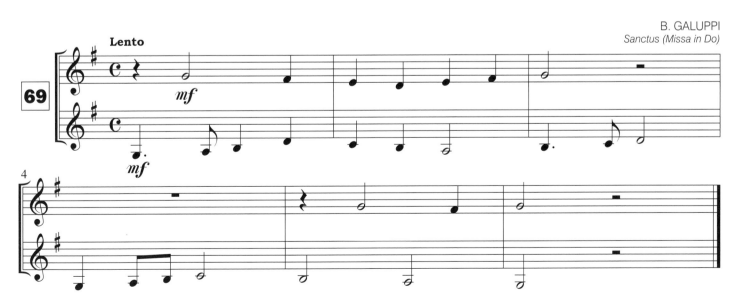

11 Melodies of 6 Notes/Rhythmic Values: from o to ♪

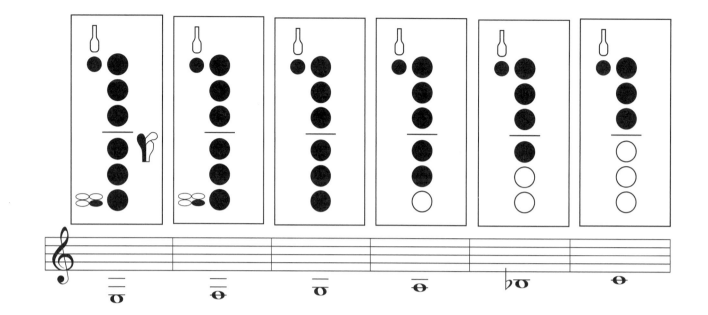

H. PURCELL (1659-1695)
A new Irish tune

Moderato

70

mf

5

W.A. MOZART
Deutsche Tänze - Serie 11 n. 13

[Allegro]

71

mf

5

A. FOOTE
Reverie

Andante

72

p

6

12

12 F-Major Scale

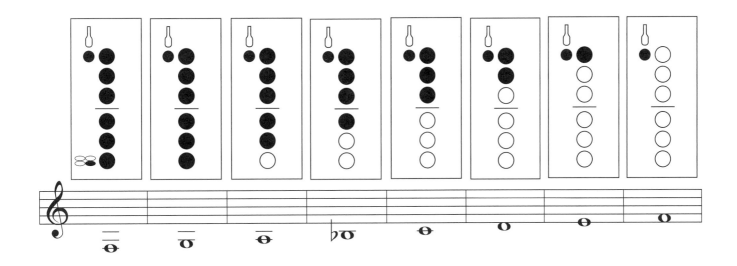

J. ROSENMÜLLER (1619-1684)
Meine Seele harret auf Gott

Presto

73

mf

M.A. CHARPENTIER
Domine Deus (Messe de minuit)

Lento

74

p

L.E. GEBHARDI (1787-1862)
2-Part canon

Moderato

75

mf

C. CZERNY
Op. 777

76 Allegretto

C. GOUNOD (1818-1893)
Gloria (Missa brevis)

77 Allegro moderato

F. BEYER
Op. 101

78 Comodo

A. CALDARA (1670-1736)
Penso e ripenso

79 Allegro

80 Moderato
p

81 Andante
mf

82 Moderato
mf

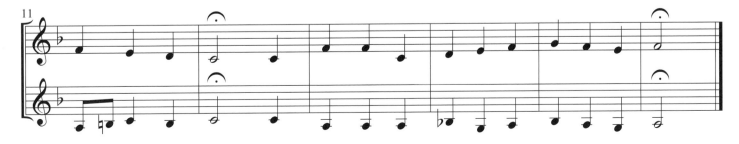

13 Melodies of 3 Notes/Rhythmic Values: 𝅝 𝅗𝅥 𝅘𝅥

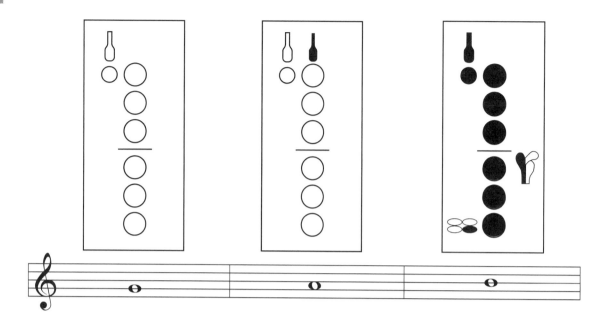

F. BEYER
Op. 101

83 Moderato

mf

K.M. KUNZ
Canons Op. 14

84 Moderato

mf

mf

K.M. KUNZ
Canons Op. 14

85 Moderato

mf

mf

14 Melodies of 4 Notes/Rhythmic Values: 𝅗𝅥. 𝅗𝅥 ♩

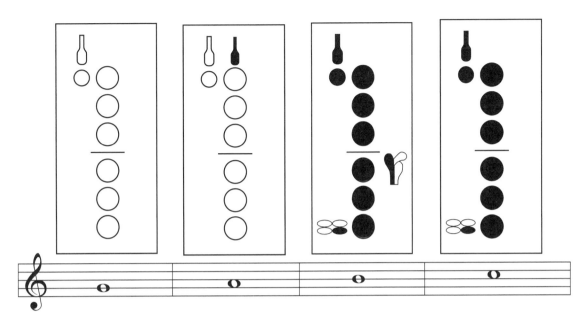

K.M. KUNZ
Canons Op. 14

Moderato

86 *mf*

mf

K.M. KUNZ
Canons Op. 14

Moderato

87 *mf*

mf

K.M. KUNZ
Canons Op. 14

Moderato

88 *mf*

mf

15 Melodies of 5 Notes/Rhythmic Values: from 𝅗𝅥. to ♪

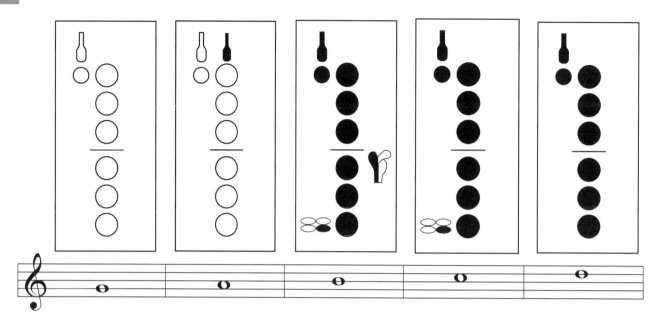

Un poco animato

A. SCHMOLL
Petit Étude

89

p

Assai vivo

A. SCHMOLL
Petit Étude

90

p

[Allegretto]

M. CORRETTE (1707-1795)
Menuet allemand

91

mf

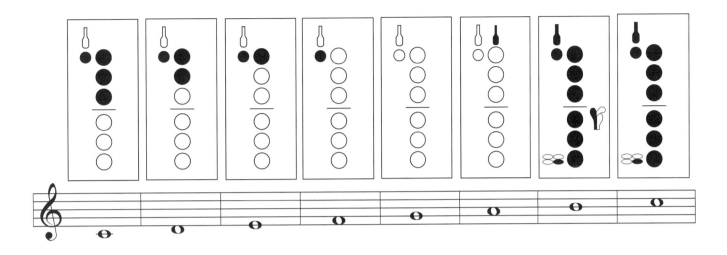

G. LANGE (1830-1889)
Arietta - Sonatina Op.114 n. 4

92 Andantino

C. FRANCK
Domine non secundum

93 Andante non troppo

I. PLEYEL
Rondò - Sonatina n. 1

94 Moderato

95 Moderato

M. HAYDN
Wie trostreich

96 Moderato

L.E. GEBHARDI
Morgengesang

97 [Andante]

L.E. GEBHARDI
Wasserlied

34

98 **Lento**

99 **Lento**

100 **Andantino**

FINGERING CHART

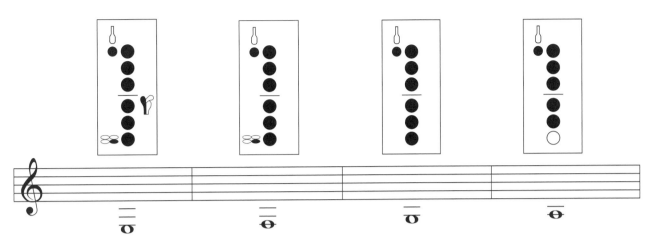

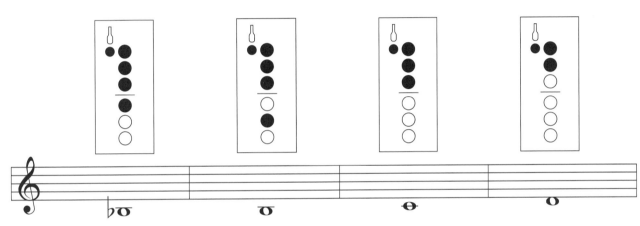

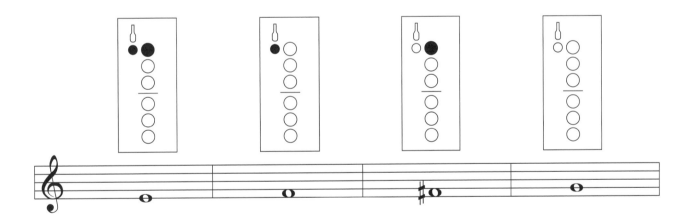

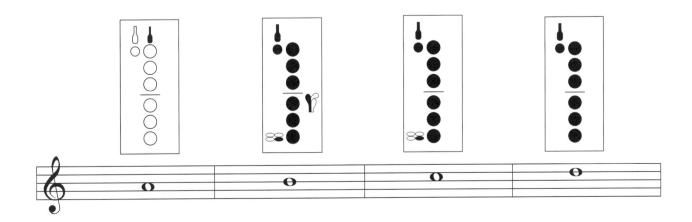

GLOSSARY

A tempo giusto	*In strict tempo*
Adagio religioso	*Slow, devotional*
Allegretto	*Fairly quick*
Allegro	*Fast*
Allegro moderato	*Moderately fast*
Andante	*Walking tempo*
Andante con moto	*Walking tempo with motion*
Andante moderato	*Moderate walking tempo*
Andante non troppo	*Walking tempo not too much*
Andantino	*Close to walking tempo*
Animato	*Animatedly*
Assai vivo	*Very lively*
Brillante e vivace	*Brilliant and lively*
Comodo	*Comfortably*
Con moto	*With motion*
Larghetto	*A little broad*
Largo	*Broad*
Lento	*Slow*
Maestoso ma non lento	*Majestic but not slow*
Melodioso	*Singing*
Menuetto grazioso	*Graceful minuet*
Moderato	*Moderately*
Molto allegro	Very quick
Non troppo veloce	*Not too rapidly*
Presto	*Very fast*
Un poco animato	*A little animated*
Vivace	*Lively*